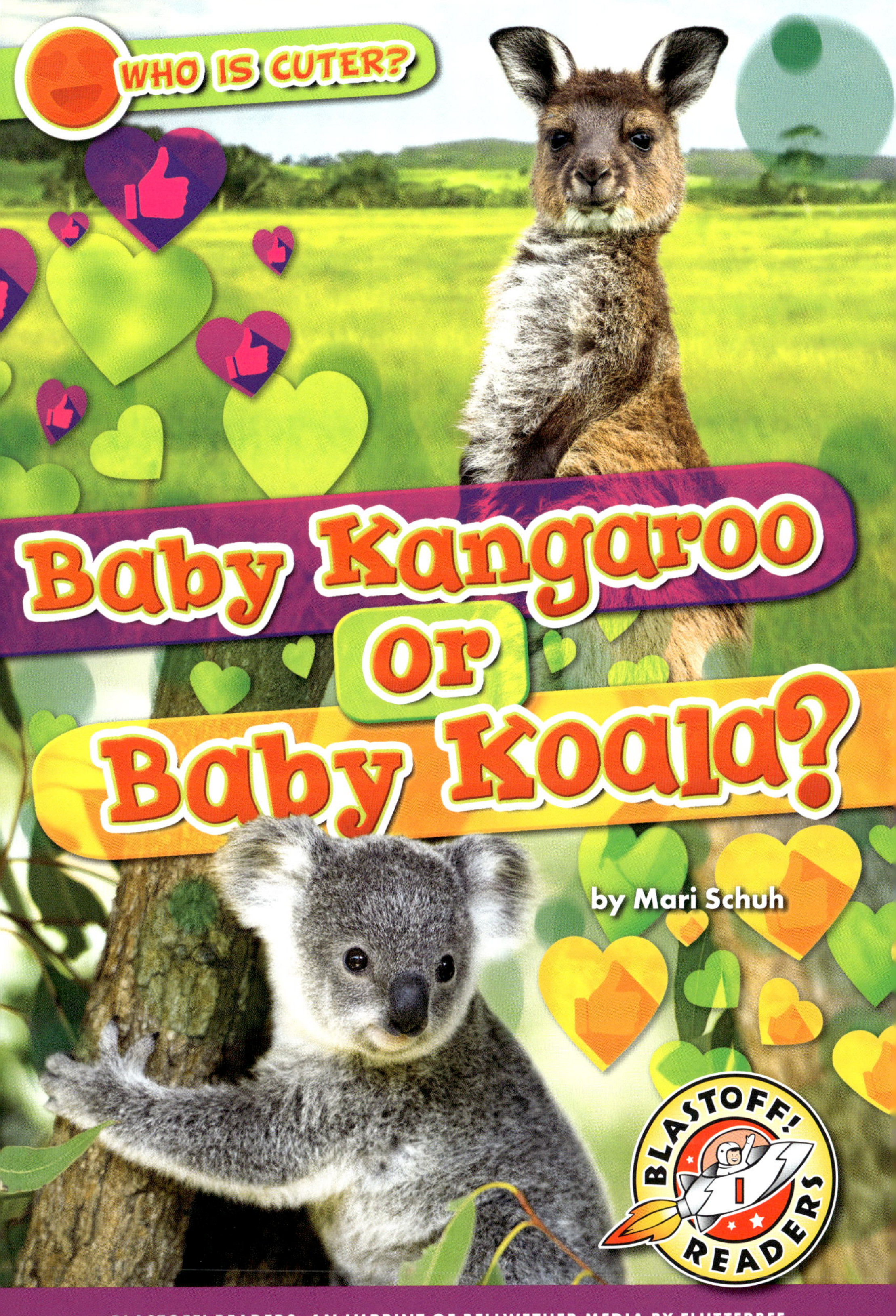

BLASTOFF! READERS: AN IMPRINT OF BELLWETHER MEDIA BY FLUTTERBEE

Blastoff! Readers are carefully developed by literacy experts to build reading stamina and move students toward fluency by combining standards-based content with developmentally appropriate text.

Level 1 provides the most support through repetition of high-frequency words, light text, predictable sentence patterns, and strong visual support.

Level 2 offers early readers a bit more challenge through varied sentences, increased text load, and text-supportive special features.

Level 3 advances early-fluent readers toward fluency through increased text load, less reliance on photos, advancing concepts, longer sentences, and more complex special features.

★ **Blastoff! Universe**

Reading Level

Grade K

Grades 1–3

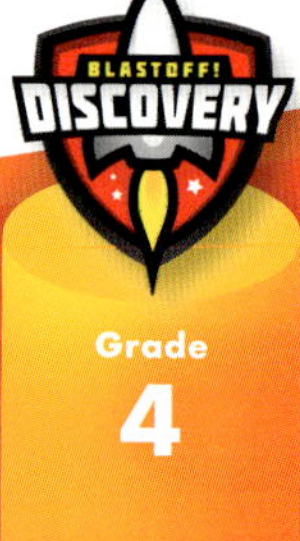

Grade 4

This edition first published in 2026 by Bellwether Media, Inc.

Library of Congress Cataloging-in-Publication Data is available at www.loc.gov or upon request from the publisher.

ISBN: 9798893047738 (hardcover)
ISBN: 9798893048735 (ebook)

Editor: Rachael Barnes

Printed in the United States of America, North Mankato, MN.

Table of Contents

Hi, Joeys!

Baby kangaroos and baby koalas share a name. They are called joeys!

kangaroo
joey
koala
joey

Newborn joeys are very small. They grow in mom's pouch.

pouch

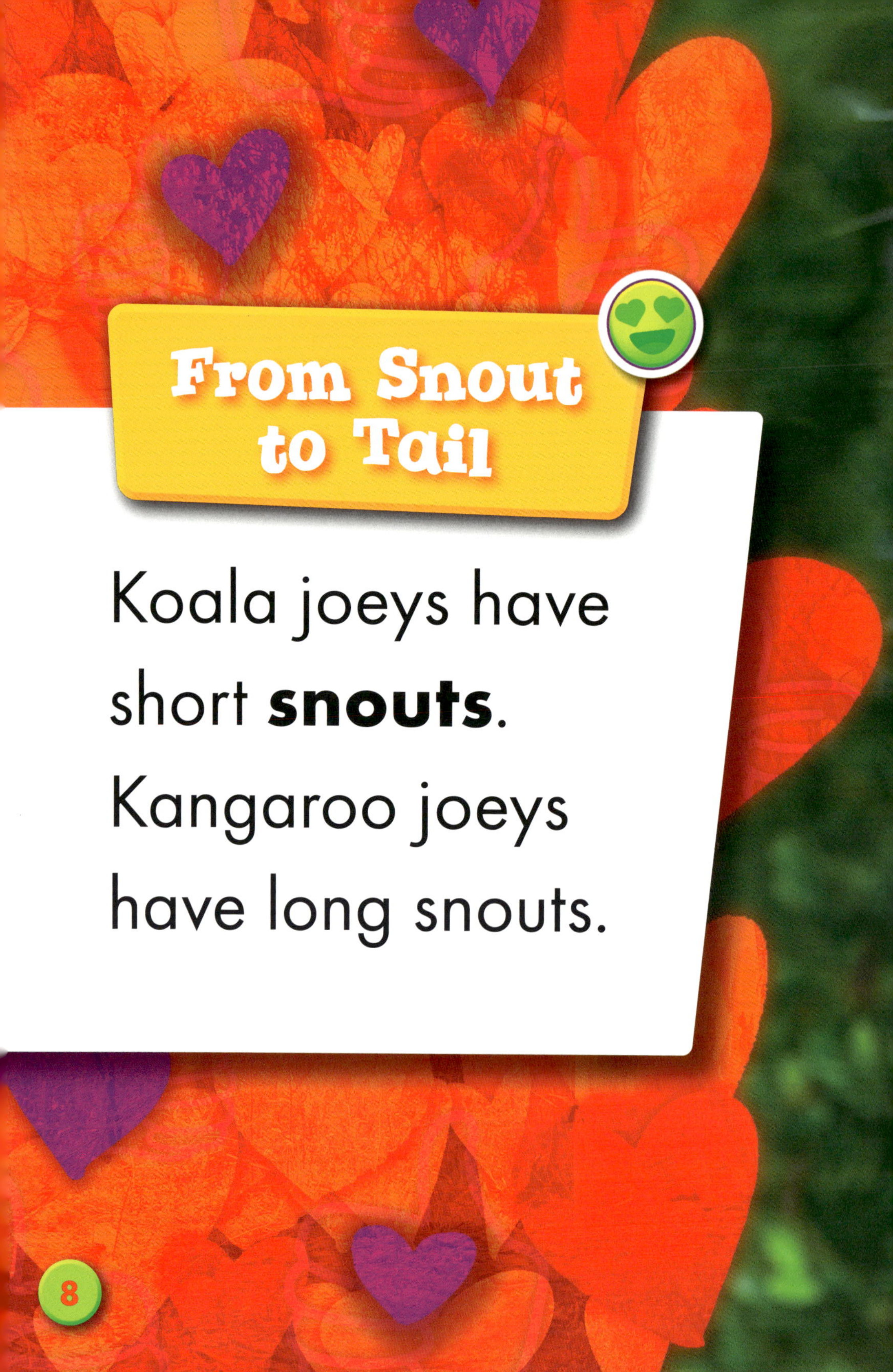

From Snout to Tail

Koala joeys have short **snouts**. Kangaroo joeys have long snouts.

short
snout
long
snout

Kangaroo joeys grow long tails. Koala joey tails are short. They are hard to see!

Kangaroo joeys grow long back legs. Koala joeys have shorter back legs.

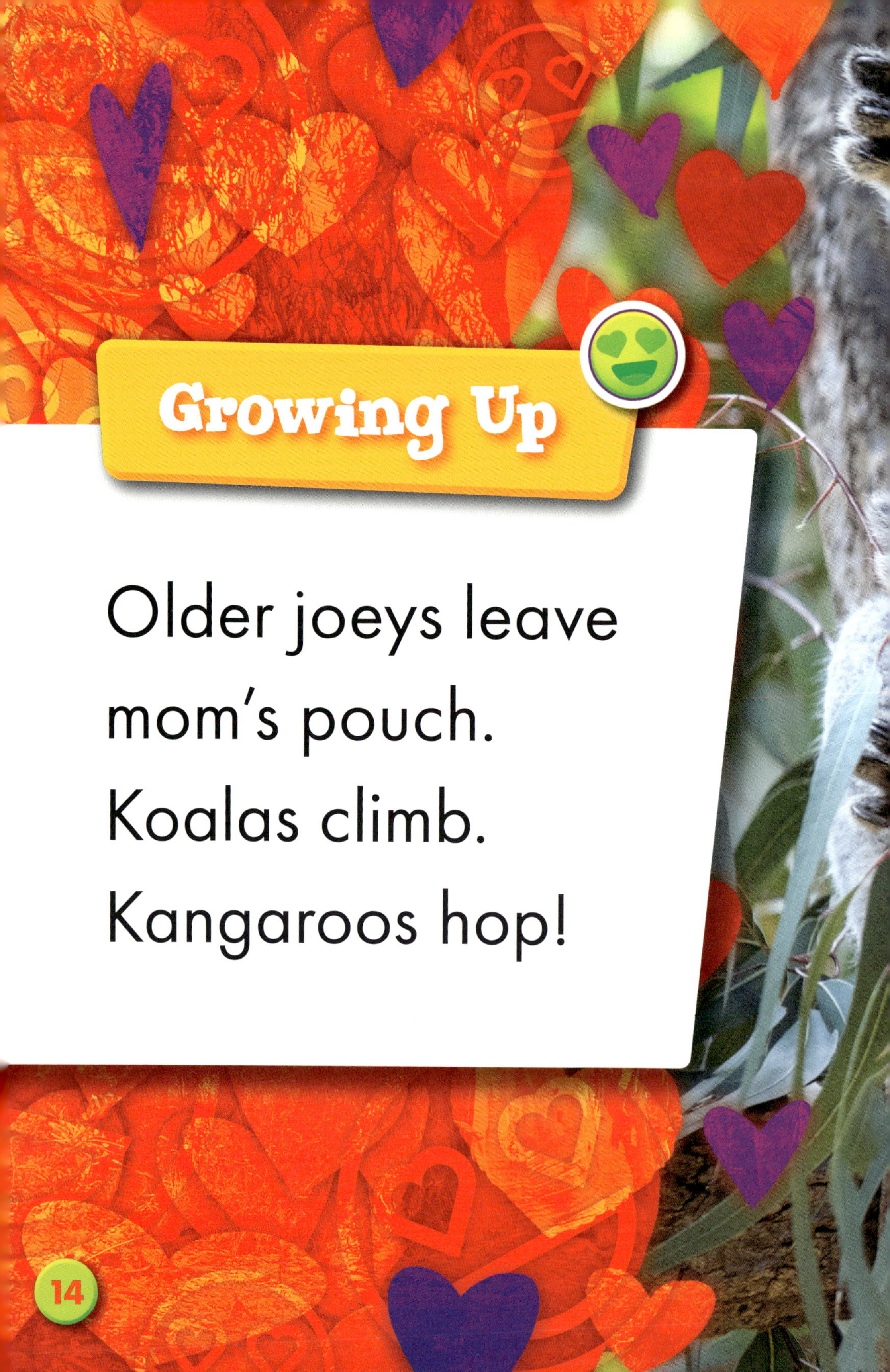

Growing Up

Older joeys leave mom's pouch. Koalas climb. Kangaroos hop!

Kangaroo joeys eat grass. Koala joeys eat **eucalyptus** leaves.

eucalyptus

Joeys grow up. Koalas often live alone. Most kangaroos live in **mobs**. Who is cuter?

mob

Who Is Cuter?
short tail
short snout
shorter back legs
Baby Koala
climbs
eats eucalyptus leaves
often lives alone

Who is your pick?
Vote at
BellwetherMedia.com
long
snout
long tail
long
back legs
Baby Kangaroo
hops
eats grass
lives in a
mob

Glossary

eucalyptus

related to a type of shrub or tree that grows in Australia and nearby islands

newborn

only just born

mobs

groups of kangaroos

snouts

the noses and mouths of some animals

To Learn More

AT THE LIBRARY

Nilsen, Genevieve. *Koala Joeys.* Minneapolis, Minn.: Jump!, 2022.

Noel, Kari. *Guess the Marsupial.* Minneapolis, Minn.: Gray Duck Creative Works, 2020.

Rustad, Martha E.H. *All About Baby Koalas.* North Mankato, Minn.: Pebble, 2022.

ON THE WEB

FACTSURFER

Factsurfer.com gives you a safe, fun way to find more information.

1. Go to www.factsurfer.com.
2. Enter "baby kangaroo or baby koala" into the search box and click 🔍.
3. Select your book cover to see a list of related content.

Index

The images in this book are reproduced through the courtesy of: Signature Message, front cover (plains background); Wonderly Imaging, front cover (kangaroo); Andras Deak, front cover (koala); Enrico Della Pietra, background (throughout); Michael Evans, background (throughout); Libby, background (throughout); Animal Search, p. 3 (koala); hamid300, p. 3 (kangaroo); Andrew Haysom/ Getty Images, pp. 4-5; stanciuc, p. 5; picture alliance/ Contributor/ Getty Images, pp. 6-7; DEA/ C.DANI/ I.JESKE/ Contributor/ Getty Images, p. 7; Rosie Leaney/ Getty Images, pp. 8-9; worldswildlifewonders, p. 9; markrhiggins, pp. 10-11; Bossa Art., p. 11; Tomas Lesa, pp. 12-13; Molyomoto, p. 13; lastpresent, pp. 14-15; Ilya Postnikov, p. 15; Chansom Pantip, p. 16; Cavan, pp. 16-17; tracielouise/ Getty Images, p. 17; daphot75, pp. 18-19, 20 (climbs); Maria Kazakova1, p. 19; Eric Isselee, p. 20 (koala); Freder, p. 20 (eats leaves); manuk74, p. 20 (lives alone); Sean Burges/ Alamy Stock Photo, p. 21 (kangaroo); Bradley Blackburn, p. 21 (hops); Lea Scaddan/ Getty Images, p. 21 (eats grass); AscentXmedia, p. 21 (lives in mob); Roxana, p. 22 (eucalyptus leaves); slowmotiongli, p. 22 (mobs); Jami Tarris/ Getty Images, p. 22 (newborn); Gary, p. 22 (snouts).